Prism

Catching Seisms of Life

Akanksha

Dedication

To all those who are trying to conquer their fears , their pain and their anguish towards the spins of this wheel of life. I urge them to keep faith in there own self.

Preface

Being from a technical field , I never ever thought that there would be a time when I will have a basket of poems of my own pen, where each and every fruit of it would have been grown by myself.

It was never under my plan to write something, anything that could even have a single audience to read. But life has its own road with different turns and each turn being unique in its constructions and in its attributes. Each have its own ups and downs. Each have its own share of trees to give its wayfarers a chance to rest under its shade and have a kinky bite of its fruits.

While journeying farers experience a gradience of emotions. While for some a teeny tiny pond is enough to quench their thirst but for the others it takes a river alongside the road to experience that seventh heaven.

This collection set is nothing but a milieu of experiences through which a layman passes in that unique span of time that god has offered to them. While taking a ride through this book it is possible that the poem to which one rider might feel connected is different to other rider.

So the poems are those reaped fruits that wanted to get tasted by every soul of god's creation.

Acknowledgements

For this marvellous creation there are some of the most important people to whom I would like to acknowledge.

First one being my mother and father, who always believed in me and said "Do what you think is right".

Then my husband Anshuman, who always believed in the fact that whatever one wants to do in life should make one happy and satisfied with one's work. As for him the real treasure lies in complacency.

The next stop of my journey as a poet was fulfilled by my little sister Akshita, who although younger to me but I do not remember when did she become my support system in whatever decision I took.

The last one being none other but I, Me, Myself......My complete self. As it is a real tough task to take a different road than that usually other people take. Then sticking to that path inspite of the struggles needs a high flame heated iron like courage and determination. I hope people find this strength and power after reading this book.

1. Memento, The Nostalgic Piece

Down, Down, Down again
Closed my eyes
In order to gain
In order to loose
In order to rise
Through my vice again,

Was I the one
Who shot a hockey goal
Was I the one who shot a bullet in the hole
Was I the one who got her hands raised
Was I the one who wanted to do it all

None, none, none to condemn
Just rewinding the pages of life again

I lost my way
While paddling away
I went far

Far too, too far
In the search of a stone
Unknowingly hidden in my home

Adrift, puzzled, bewildered now I
lay on my bed searching who am I
Tears welled in my eyes
While collecting the mementoes of my life.

2. The Wandering Soul

Knock knock oh hell
Just open the door
I have come from the heaven
Let me come indoor

Furious doorkeeper asked
How come you call us
Hell in a whole

I told him my story
I was dragged on a lorry
I was served to seven
As a meal of intoxication

My whole life was gone
I was left to die alone

For million years oh heaven
The nymphs have been serving
Leaving their masters often

Peeved, piqued, disgruntled somewhere
While I served my masters
In a night alone

Now I have come
To ask, To decide, To settle
If I have come
To the hell or a heaven

I am nothing
But a wandering soul
Likewise there are many more
Queued up to knock your door

3. Nerve

Today is the day
Of my confessions
I reached out to them
With an obscure possession

At the first hand
I breathe, breathe, breathe
Vayu came into picture you see
I told him my fear
Of being stormed out by him
He said anger is the demon
Not him, not him

Dragged out by Vayu
Bhumi took control of my feet
Grappling, wrestling, fighting me
I come on the surface
With the fear of being caught again
She said anger is the demon
Not her, not her

Parched and varied I
Reached the serene Apas nearby
The babbling stream, the chirping birds
Might be a sight for sore eyes
I was laughing, giggling inside my head
When the sudden torrent flushed me ahead
She said anger is the demon
Not her, not her

Faltering, stumbling, staggering me
Reaching my abode to get some sleep
But the destination turned into a well of death
By the Akash burning down with its flesh

By the by
I got the sight of Agni
Burning my nest
They said anger is the demon
Not them, not them

I am blank in my soul
With nothing left

4. The Coerce Stone

One twilight I closed my eyes
Pondering over the rising sun to come
Tossing and turning and piping dreams
When a power of ominiscience came into being

An unforeseen sight took me into sanity
I found worried souls, not single but more

I felt an unhappy lad for a hundredth ball
I felt a restless student with an inferior marks
juggling with the fear of being caught along

The exhausted father had a burdened soul
as his head was dipped deep into hole of debt
The disechantment of two-some
The unfulfilled demands of marital halves
Lets slip to count how many whistles does the cooker
got

Waking up, hitting the sack

Waking up, hitting the sack
The rivalries with oneself keep going on

The untamed desire to soar high
When parting the soul from the mortal aside
Leads to nothing in the end
But a coerced stone which was
Trying to get refinement all along

5. The Templeless Town

Often I wonder for
The primitives who created
The temple, The Church
The Mosque, all the synagogues
The question of need arises in all

Whilst it have the serenity
For the wearied man in the street
But now and then disagreements
Turn these serenities into a holy war
Ah! What the terrible sight the god cry

Whilst by menifestation itself
Joe Blow got a sleep of heaven
But eventually the festivities
Rip off the joy of guarding hands
Ah! What the terrible sight the god cry

Whilst it obliviates the pain
The rage, the anguish through the soul

But further the arosen secrilege
Turns them into a quarrelsome more
Ah! What the terrible sight the god cry

Then Kabira rises, Rahim rose
Nanak arises for a single thing
Wouldn't it have been better
If there is no single such thing
The Nirguna, The Formless, The Soulbearer
Lives in the heart, need no more temple

6. Playing The Protagonist

In the wee hours of the day
The old almighty master picked
A pair of canvas and a brush
To draw a picture

The dexterous, The dauber
Had his choices so crafty
While he shaded one in a golden white
Another was tinctured with a brownish khaki

While one was surrounded with a settling aurora
Another was shown with a lower horizon
While one was delivered as a born personality
Another was left with a struggling reality

Since the grain have found the name of their eaters
A mole to be drawn is left behind
To find who is its go getter

The artsy craftsy two came alive

They started sharing a conjugal vibe
They pulled up their brushes
They pulled on their gears
Started casting their respective fates

No one was proud, no one was loud
But the weaker pulled the sword higher
No night no day being one and similar

Eventually the mole started taking its place
It turned into a sun brighter than its face
It got stick into the forehead for the time unknown
Leaving a lesson behind alone

No birth, No stealing
No inheritance, nothing at all
What works for one is hard work and all
Almighty have a marked place
For those determined to leave a mark on their own

7. Bloom

Oh rusty, stained, dirty window
On the run-off-the-mill I see you
Silently I stand engulfing
The noise I am surrounded by
Silently I stand gazing
Over the attires they wore
Silently I stand pondering
Over the wrinkles on their forehead
They got by the time passing by
Thier hands, their feet
Their Posture, Thier burden
That they carry on their jostles
The hurry, the rush
The bundle of the bush
keeps more and more push
Until breathe is in their possession
I am nothing but the petal
Of the same flower like them
Which blossoms and blooms
From summer to winter

Until autumn sheds their
Life in a single flitter

8. Jhuni

Caressing the body of her lover
The girls was sat near a shovel
The grave was dug deep
But her heart reluctant
To let him go to an eternal sleep

Jhuni, Oh Jhuni! My beloved
Whispered the voice from behind
Step back and observe
The soul not here anymore
The spirit might
Have taken another form
The body that you are holding
Nothing but a carcass
In dire need to conform

Oh Brother! Oh Brother!
The persistent pain
Is aching the heart
Longing to reunite

Only time can heal
Your broken heart, Oh Dear!
But your sinking may
Bring your wheel to an end

Let it move rather slowly
With its cukoo around, Oh Jhuni!
Let the melancholy go, Oh Jhuni!

9. Chapati

Honking horns, running cars
Speeding buses, fumes all over
Sitting under the bridge
Spreading my hands over
I am a begger, I am a begger

How breackneck, how expeditious
How fleet the survival has become

My eyes have swollen
My feets have corn
My body has boiled
Under the burning sun
I have marks all over except one
I am a begger , I am a begger

Let me be with my scars Oh God!
But add to it one more
On my hands , in my mouth
In my throat, under my bloated gut

The scar made by a hot Chapati
Nothing more, nothing more

10. Nirvana

Devinity once asked
Don't you want this
Rough road to surpass
An exceptional light
From within replied

I am born as Akanksha
I am born to be Akanksha
I am the desire
Longings of the people
Thrive through me
How can you border me
Vis an act to flee

No Moksha, No Deliverance
No Redemption, No Escape is as pleasant
As incredible mother earth
And her cuddly lap
Is where I want to be

The beaming, shining
Radiance I found
Captivated by the charm
Of the folks around
Proffer me something, anything better
I am born to be Akanksha
Here is my Nirvana
Hitherto Desire

11. Hey Nani

Wrinkled but soft
Ageing and warm fingers
Running through my hairs
Are some fond and precious
Summers that I had

Her stories through my ears
Some fables some real
With my Nana as hero
But not her as his better half
Are etched throughout my past

Her threaded spectacles
Often ran from her nose
Upto her head picking
Teeny tiny little bugs
Through a plate of raw rice

Most often she was tight lipped
With a diffident smile

But when my mother came to take me
Frowned gloom filled her eyes
These are some fond and precious
Summers that I had

12. Well of Fables

On the periphery of this village
Resides a deep well with its
Infamous fables of being a spooky hell

Besides the well lies a bald tree
Taking position as a kneeled warrior
With a sword in his hand being a valorous gladiator

When its dark and gloomy
The soothing voice of rustling leaves
Turns into an eerie chilling howling of a dark beast

The warm smoke around rises
A little upto the sky
Creating an ominous shadow alive

Caught in an open dilemma now I
To reach my destination
Its the only way to ride, Alas!
Its the grizzly way to ride, Alas!

13. The Encounter

It was cold , It was night
Filled with a soul chilling vibe
I heard the footsteps
Sometimes low paced , sometimes fast
The shutters were down
No trolley, no carts around
My heart was thumping, bumping
Thrown into panic all deep down
My soul was running
But my feet were stumbling
My blood through my veins
Started rising high to my brains
But the sudden clotted eyes
Started feeling its melt down
When the stranger passed by my side
Leaving me numb and
Beatless in this peculiar ride
That night I felt the cry of the deer
The arousal of fear
Out of the chase by the tiger

Her pain her struggles of
being tore into pieces
Leaving me collapsed in my whole self

15. Acoustics of My Childhood

One early morning
Mother wrapped me up
With a small paper pocket
Full of worthy stuff

She asked me to open it up
When no one is around
Especially father, as his likings
To keep us ground

A young, artless, naive lass was I
Obeyed my mother
No question, no doubt there was

As a girl living in her boarding
I was onboard for a ride
With a load of backpacks
Placed by my side

Puff! Puff! Puff!
Tangled hairs, jerks up and down
Got a sudden brake
To an end of the line

I reached my hostel, a room in line
Opened up the pouch
That my mother wanted me to have
No, No, No was not just a pouch
But a letter tied together
With some extra bucks to survive

"Listen dear daughter
You listen me well
Use your money thoughtfully
Its not just a paper
But a hard earned money
By your dear dad
Cravings for money has no end
But craving for your goals
Will give you a stand out in all
Remember, distinction of glimpses
Of a lion and a pack of dogs." Mother wrote

The golden words got etched
Through my soul, to my bit of nails

15. Pepper and Salt

A peculiar mirage hit me
Like an uninvited guest
Peeping into my inspirations
Through the canopies of the window
When my eyes got deceived
Of a grey haired lock
Wreigning over my face
It sent me into a galaxy
Of stars filled with unfulfilled fantasies

There were a house on a hill
Surrounded with cluster of neem
Some bamboos and apple trees all around
Scent of the soil filling my nostrils
After rain giving me a boohoo in a while
The grey haze covered my house
Finally giving it a touch
Of the lap of heaven
Where I am resting by
When the snow starts falling

Some beautiful visitors arrive
A wolf or a bear taking a sight
On me through my glassdoor
Is cherry on top for a wanderer rusting by

16. Tangled

A little torn off bridge of silence
Has tied the two
No other but my mother in law and me
Sometimes I wanted to get a hold on to it
But now allowed to

This strange and grizzly while
Catching a serene vibe
Being far apart in our natal days
Her being a septugenerian sage
While me a tricenarian qualified

Often her astonishing push
To break the fetters around me
Tied by the alphas long ago
But next comes my covered face
In the garb of the great old
Culture to be soared

Often, but next

Often, but next
Tangled, ensnared, netted
A bird caught between
Her liberty and the enchanting gold cage

What rests between the two
The incessant, the unceasing
A tangled silence
Waiting to be broke in a unison

17. Saatuki

Once upon a time
Vishnu incarnated as Rama
Who drove all traits of Vishnu
Except of being an omniverse manipulator
As Rama had humility in its earnest form

The exemplary son left
His own wealth, his own throne
For the sake of fulfilment of his father's vow
Even not a tinge of bitterness in his heart
Oh my poor son! Kaushalya cried

It was Lakshmi who had already felt the naive soul
Arrived in the mould of Sita
To be Rama's charioteer
How could such an innocent soul
Would kill the cunning Raavana at all

Sita being the saatuki
Also became the driving mole

A deer being golden
Just a mirage, nothing at all

Was Rama unacquaint
Was Sita unacquaint
This was time to break free
The mirage of Ravana as a whole

The saatuki Sita and the Rama faced Arjuna
Is all in my knowledge has evolved

18. A mirror to fear

How does this fear looks like
Is he taller or shorter
Is he thicker or thinner
Is he long haired or bob done
Is he prettier or ugly
Is he really a he
Or a little bit filled with a she

My heart fills with astonishment
When I assign it a face
My heart feels mercy
When I know where he lives
When I know where he comes from
He is no where around
But inside the corner of my heart
Just a tap, he is out

Untangling my fetters
I asked him once
Have you ever seen

A mountain, a river or a sea?
Have you ever been in woods
With his feet stuck in deep
Have you ever stepped in a dark room
Have you ever climbed the top
Or let's make it simpler
Have you ever failed an exam
Have you ever crossed a road
Have you ever been interviewed
By an obnoxious bald man
Have you ever been in debt

"No", he said gulping within himself
Tiny, tiny, tiny he begun to get nowhere
But a mirror was shown to himself

19. A shame plant

I was thoughtful one sunset
Decided to water all my plants

They were all lined up
Ready to get their shares
Like a numb, innocent, thirsty lad

It was a sprawling, teeming, eye-catching sight
Wondered never put my foot
My heart was asking by and by

From the medicative neem
To the savouring aam
I rain them all over
With a cane of bursting cloud

Eventually a little sapling
Caught me by surprise
It was a prickly long lived
Shame plant started to shrink by

What pink and fluffy petals it had
Alas! It took me into the world
Of my beautiful little girl
That once I had

I wish through my core
Oh Almighty! Like this plant
Make every girl on this plant
Sensitive and armouring
That any sore eyed man
Could not have dared her
In his loftiest blink

Oh Almighty! Make the soul
Of the shame plant rest into them
What a wonderful shield
Then they would have

20. The Singing Butterfly

Mingled muses, mise-en-scene
Perched a bumble bee by my side
Wings filled with an aura
Of a dusky setting sun
Striped as in waining
Moon of a pure dark night
With a flamboyant moustache
Of a reigning monarch
Flaps the wing as a royal mantle
Ready to address all the vice
Although a warrior in the creation
But gentle in the mental
Clicks and sings in an angelic voice

"Oh my lovely lovely petal!
You are so soft and gentle
You have given me a life
So calm and so humble
My euphoria of your love
Keeps on rising

When the nectar of your soul
Becomes the chassis of vehicle"

21. Little Escapes

The scenario happened
While her plucking the flower
From a leaning tower
I landed a hand
By the god's grace
But god gave me a lesson in that place
Suddenly I lost my control
My legs left their mould
The polka music started playing around
My breathe goes up
The counting goes on
The mortal clock started ticking along
I could not find the sky
I could not find me down
Now I was hanging up above the ground
Between heaven and earth
I found my mirth
How my escapes does one gets in life
On the road, by the bus
In the night, with the flesh and blood

By the air, under the water
By the sea, or the mountain
Or just inside the house?